Boys 2 MENtors™

Boys 2 MENtors™

STUDENT WORKBOOK

GIRL FRIDAY BOOKS

Copyright © 2022 The Leadership Program

All rights reserved.

No part of this book may be reproduced, or stored in a retrieval system, or transmitted in any form or by any means, electronic, mechanical, photocopying, recording, or otherwise, without express written permission of the publisher.

Published by The Leadership Program, New York
www.theleadershipprogram.com

The Leadership Program
535 8th Avenue, Floor 16
New York, NY 10018

Published by Girl Friday Books™, Seattle
www.girlfridaybooks.com

Produced by Girl Friday Productions

ISBN 978-1-959411-02-4

Printed in the United States of America

Welcome to Boys 2 MENtors™! In this book you will have the opportunity to express your thoughts, feelings, and opinions about issues that are relevant to your life today and to your future vision of yourself.

These pages offer a variety of activities, with options to express yourself in diverse formats, including helpful information pages, guided worksheets, and "Scribble or Sketch" pages for you to free write or draw on your own. All together they'll provide you an opportunity to record, sketch, capture, digest, list, absorb, and reflect on your Boys 2 MENtors™ journey. We hope you enjoy the ride!

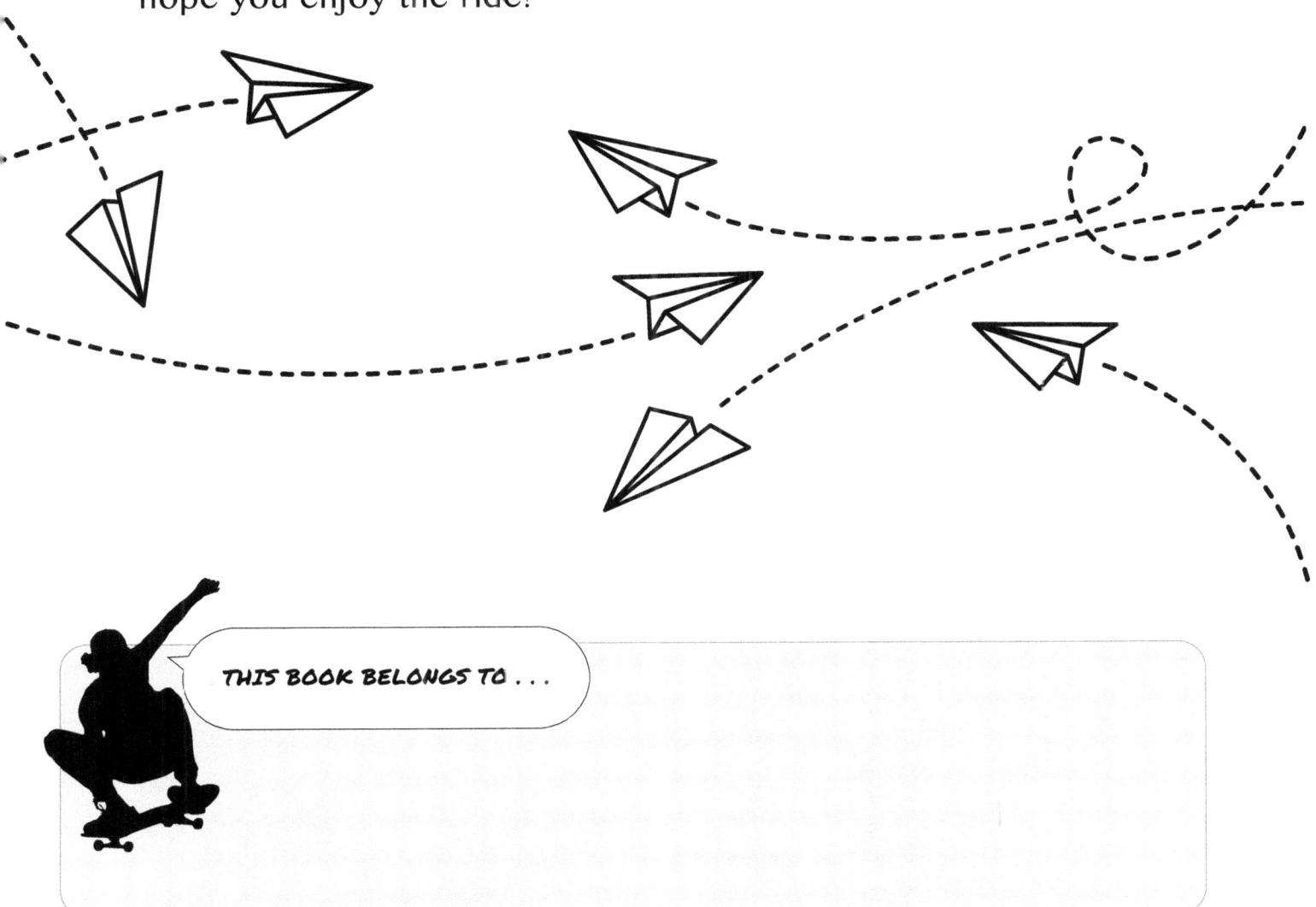

THIS BOOK BELONGS TO . . .

Contents

Section One: Lead Up / Introduction

Personal Values *Scribble or Sketch!* 2
Setting SMART Goals 3
Leadership Contract 4
Goal Grid 5
The Ideal Role Model Leader 6

Section Two: What's Up? / Identity

Why I Am the Way I Am 8
Personality Goes a Long Way 10
Around My Way 12
T-Shirt Slogan 14
Walk Down Their Block 15
Sample Figure 16
Healthy Body Image *Scribble or Sketch!* 17
Biography of a Stranger 18
Making Impressions *Scribble or Sketch!* 19

Section Three: Step Up / Interacting

Active Listening Behavior 22
Active Listening Detective 23
Hint, Hint 24
Perception Picture 25
Society's Perceptions *Scribble or Sketch!* 26
Dealing with Stereotypes and Bias 27
Self-Care *Scribble or Sketch!* 28
My Many Roles 29
Role Analysis 30
Relationship Web 31
Who's the Man? 32
Lyric Breakdown 33
What Constitutes a Healthy Relationship 34
Unhealthy Relationship Warning Signs! 35
How to Talk So Trusted Adults Will Listen 36

Section Four: Own Up / Personal Responsibility

Say What?..38
Medals of Compassion..39
The Torch of Compassion Burns Strong..............................40
Opinion Influences *Scribble or Sketch!*..........................41
Declaration of Respect for Girls and Women........................42
Portrait to Image Sample..43
Ideas + Images..44
What's My Style?..45
Tease My Brain..48
My Backpack...49
What's the Message?...50
Twinkle, Twinkle, Little Star.....................................51
Learning Styles: What Kind of Learner Are You?....................52
Action Plan in Action Example.....................................54
Action Plan in Action...55
My Ideal Neighborhood...56
What's Your Plan for Change?......................................57
Immediate Actions, Long-Term Effects..............................58
School Service Takeover Tasks.....................................59
Community Service *Scribble or Sketch!*...........................60

Section Five: Man Up / My Roles as a Man

What's in a Name?...62
My Favorite TV Dad..63
HisStory Profile..64
My Vision Statement...65
The Five Worlds of Success..66
Successful Man *Scribble or Sketch!*..............................67
Talking to Authority Figures *Scribble or Sketch!*................68
Dealing with Disappointment *Scribble or Sketch!*.................69
Speaking with Authority Figures...................................70

Section Six: Rise Up / Future Plans

Responding to Failure *Scribble or Sketch!*.......................72
No Problem! Sample Problem..73
No Problem!...74
Choices, Decisions, Consequences (Sample Model)...................75
To Blank or Not to Blank..76

    C, D, C—Setting the Scene 77
    What's My Goal? 78
    How Do I Get Where I'm Going? 79
    Pyramid of Success 81
    Vision Page 82
    My Ideal Roommate 83
    Dream Job Requirements 85
    Career Pursuit 86
    Ideal Legacy *Scribble or Sketch!* 87
    Dream Image Job Opening 88
    Interview Dos and Don'ts 89
    Final Reflections *Scribble or Sketch!* 90

Reference

    Credits 92
    About The Leadership Program 93

Lead Up/ Introduction

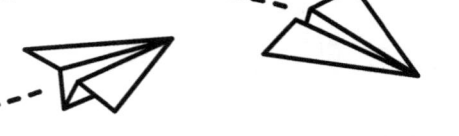

PERSONAL VALUES SCRIBBLE OR SKETCH!
(use this space to write or draw your thoughts and feelings about **personal values to live by**)

SETTING SMART GOALS

Long-range goals point you in the right direction to achieve what really matters most in your life.

For example, "I want to graduate from high school with honors."

Intermediate goals show you how to do it. Intermediate goals are easier to reach if you break them into smaller steps.

For example, "I need to get a B average this semester in my English class in order to achieve my long-range goal." These goals are reached when they become part of our daily task.

Daily tasks tell us what we have to do today to achieve our long-range and intermediate goals.

For example, "I need to read my English assignment for three hours today from 5:00 to 8:00 p.m."

When you begin to set goals be sure they are SMART goals:

Specific:	An unwritten goal is merely a wish. Writing the goal forces you to be specific. State exactly what will be accomplished. If a goal is not specific, you will have a hard time knowing whether you've reached it.
Measurable:	You only improve what you measure. If you set a goal that can't be easily measured, such as "Be more honest," chances are you won't make much improvement.
Action-Oriented:	Set up things to be done. Goals should always focus on actions, rather than personal qualities. Instead of having the goal "I will do my homework every day," write about specific actions. "I will complete my homework every day from 4:00 to 5:30 p.m. at the desk in my room."
Realistic:	Goals must be realistic. It's good to aim high, but if we aim too high, we can get discouraged, and the goal-setting process can become just another fruitless activity. On the other hand, goals that are too easily reached are just as useless and unrealistic as goals that are too far beyond our reach.
Timely:	Be sure that the time allowed is reasonable. Goals must be timely. Don't set a goal for which you honestly don't have time right now. And don't give yourself so much time that the goal becomes meaningless.

NAME: _____

LEADERSHIP CONTRACT

DATE _____

I, _____, as a member of The Leadership Program, agree to achieve the following **class** goals:

_____
_____
_____
_____
_____
_____
_____
_____
_____
_____
_____
_____
_____

As an individual, I agree to achieve the following **personal** goal(s):

_____
_____
_____
_____
_____
_____

Signed _____ Witness _____

Witness: Each member of the class must choose a witness to his contract. Choose the witness carefully. The witness is a person who agrees to support you throughout the sessions. The witness congratulates and celebrates steps toward the achievement of the goal with you. If you are having difficulty achieving the goal, the witness listens, supports, reviews, and evaluates modifications to the goal with you.

NAME:

GOAL GRID

Category	Most difficult to achieve or follow	Ideas to be successful
Ground Rule		
Class Goal		
Personal Goal		

NAME: _____

THE IDEAL ROLE MODEL LEADER

A) List the **qualities** of an ideal role model leader.

B) **Prioritize** each quality as:
   Vital, Important, or Nice to have.

C) **Rate** yourself against each quality on a scale from 1 to 5:
   1=Poor, 2=Fair, 3=Average, 4=Very Good, 5=Outstanding.

(A) Quality	(B) Priority	(C) Rate

What leadership qualities do you possess?

In what situations or places do you use your leadership abilities?

What's Up? / Identity

NAME: _____

WHY I AM THE WAY I AM

You are who you choose to be, but your personality—what makes you you—comes from how you're raised and what you've picked up from the world around you. Personality goes a long way. What's yours?

PART 1:
In the space below, list some of the parts of your personality that are specific and peculiar to you (e.g., your sense of humor, the way your mind works, your sense of style).

Personality:

NAME:

PART 2:
Looking at some of the characteristics you wrote down, think about where these aspects of your personality may have come from.

In the space below, divide each of your personality traits into one of the following two categories: Raised with It (traits associated with your birth and family) and Picked It Up (what you've adapted from your community, your school, your neighborhood, television, movies, fashion, and so on).

The Way I Am

Raised with It:

Picked It Up:

NAME: _____

PERSONALITY GOES A LONG WAY

Some personality traits you're born or raised with.
Some you pick up along the way.

Fill in the columns below to rate the traits of your personality—which traits you like, which you wish you could change, and where you think they came from.

Personality traits I like about myself	Where I think they came from
1.	
2.	
3.	
4.	
5.	

Personality traits I wish I could change about myself	Where I think they came from
1.	
2.	
3.	
4.	
5.	

NAME:

PERSONALITY GOES A LONG WAY

1. How can you maintain the personality traits you like about yourself?

2. How can you change the personality traits you don't like about yourself?

NAME: _____

AROUND MY WAY

Take a moment to think about where you are from, where you live, even the block you live on, and how all of these places influence the person that you are. Now answer the following questions:

How has living in this country influenced who you are?
_____
_____
_____

If your family is from another country, or if you have ever lived in another country, how has that influenced who you are?
_____
_____
_____

What borough do you live in? _____
How has this borough influenced who you are?
_____
_____
_____

What neighborhood do you live in? _____
How has this neighborhood influenced who you are?
_____
_____
_____

NAME: _____

What block do you live on? _____
How has your block influenced who you are?

_____
_____
_____

Which one of these influences you the most? Why?

Which one of these influences you the least? Why?

NAME:

T-SHIRT SLOGAN

Create a slogan that represents your neighborhood for a T-shirt.
Example: *Bed-Stuy Smart 'n' Fly*

NAME: _____

WALK DOWN THEIR BLOCK

Plan a trip to a neighborhood different from the one you live in (e.g., Chinatown or Harlem, if you live in New York City; Park West or Union Heights if you're in Charleston; Andersonville or Uptown if you're in Chicago). Take a moment to look for *specific* cultural representations in that community. Write down what you see (or hear or smell) that represents culture or heritage in the chart below (e.g., hip-hop record store, Ethiopian restaurant, Baptist church, 3-D graffiti).

NEIGHBORHOOD: _____

FOOD	MUSIC	FAITH
ART	CLOTHING	LANGUAGE
GAMES/PLAY	DANCE	OTHER

SAMPLE FIGURE

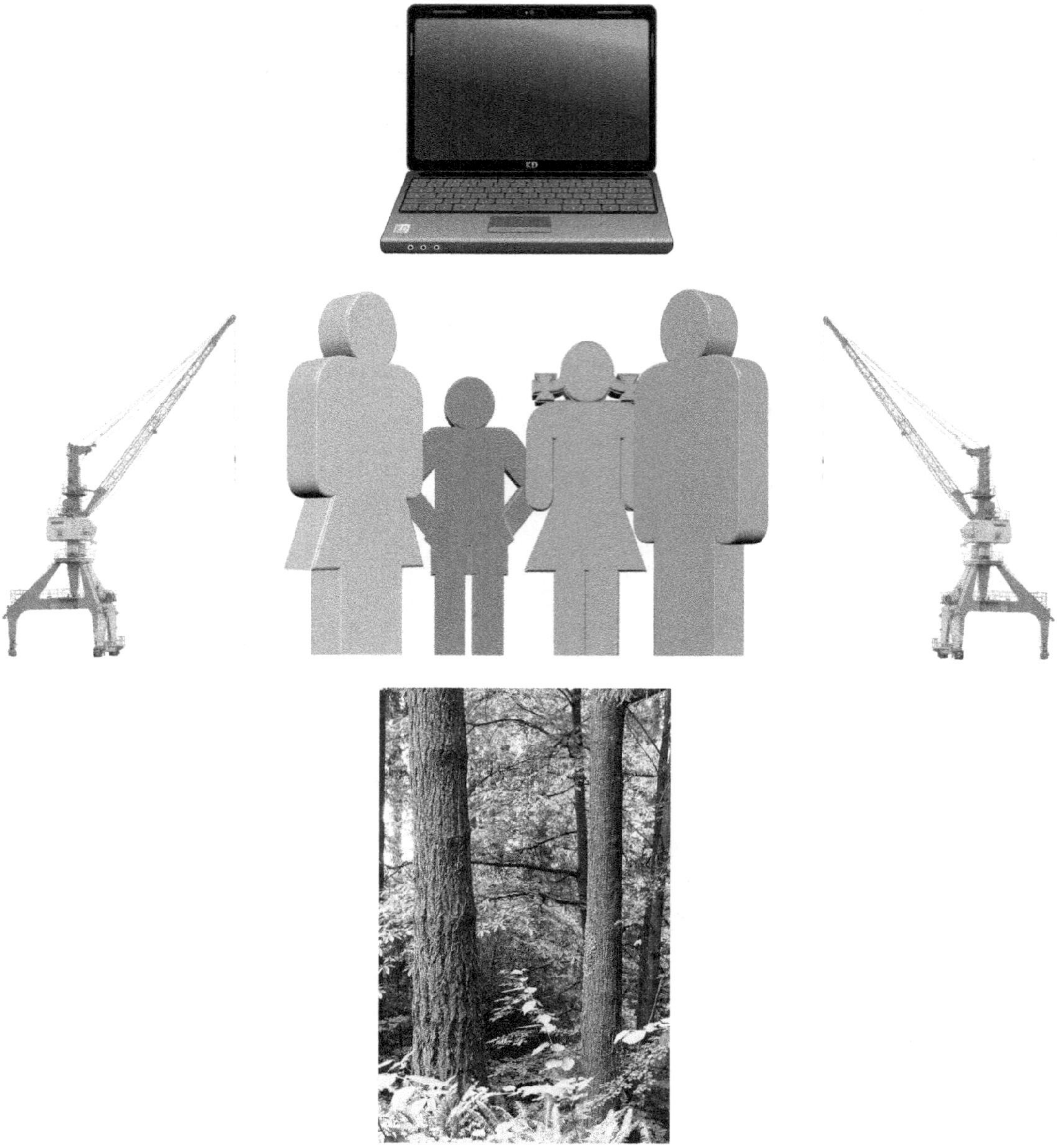

HEAD: Like a computer, full of facts and ideas

HEART: Focused on family and community

ARMS: Strong like the claws of construction cranes. Will grab on to my future and hold it tight.

LEGS: Like two trees, they will stand strong against challenges.

HEALTHY BODY IMAGE SCRIBBLE OR SKETCH!
(use this space to write or draw your thoughts and feelings about **healthy body image**)

NAME: _____

BIOGRAPHY OF A STRANGER

Choose one man in the picture you've selected, and answer the questions below about the man you have chosen. *Be specific!*

Who is this man? (Include name, age, and occupation)

What is he about to do in this picture?

What are this man's values?

How does this man spend his day?

Where does this man want to be in five years?

List five words that describe this man:

What does he want other people to think about him?

MAKING IMPRESSIONS SCRIBBLE OR SKETCH!

(use this space to write or draw your thoughts and feelings about **the impression you make on others with your clothing and appearance choices**)

Step Up / Interacting

ACTIVE LISTENING BEHAVIOR

- Look at the speaker. Make eye contact.
- Keep your body still and quiet.
- Pay attention.
- Don't interrupt.
- Watch the other person's body and face. What is his or her body saying?
- Try to understand his or her feelings, thoughts, and actions.
- Ask questions if you do not understand what they are saying.
- Listen, even if you do not like what the person is saying.
- Listen for the important points.
- _____
- _____
- _____

NAME:

ACTIVE LISTENING DETECTIVE

This week, your job is to be an active listening detective!

Your first mission is to spot one example of someone who is actively listening and one example of someone who is not.
(In your examples, describe the behaviors of the listener and the reactions from the speaker.)

Example 1:

_____
_____
_____
_____
_____

Example 2:

_____
_____
_____
_____
_____

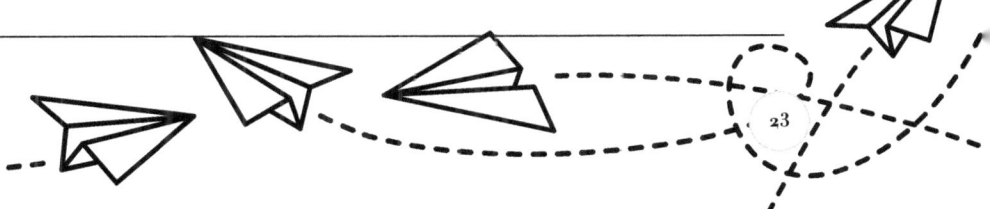

HINT, HINT

Here are some things to do that may help your communication with your parents:

- Ask them about *their* day.
- Show affection—parents want to be loved, too.
- Find out if this is a good time to talk. If it isn't,
    - be patient, and
    - ask how *you* can help *them*.
- Do your chores/homework *before* they remind you.
- Listen to them the way you would like them to listen to you.
- Let them know you appreciate what they do for you.
- Remain calm and respectful, even if you don't get the response you want.

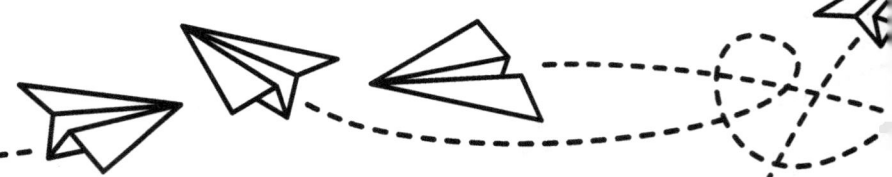

PERCEPTION PICTURE

Illustration by W.E. Hill, 1915.

SOCIETY'S PERCEPTIONS SCRIBBLE OR SKETCH!

(use this space to write or draw your thoughts and feelings about **society's perceptions of young men**)

NAME:

DEALING WITH STEREOTYPES AND BIAS

STRATEGY LIST

1. Stay calm. Try to understand where the other person is coming from.

Only engage in good-natured debates, and do not allow yourself to become defensive, which may be an instinctive reaction. Ask questions to understand how the person in front of you has developed their opinions.

2. Know when to walk away.

If you notice someone is unnecessarily combative and derogatory, withdraw from the conversation, since it will only lead to arguments and might add to negative stereotypes. Your goal isn't to change everyone's minds. That's an impossible task, so separate yourself from people who cannot engage in mature and open conversation about their opinions.

3. Stay focused on a positive objective.

Above all, try to value the differences that exist. We live in a breathtakingly beautiful world full of intelligent, interesting, and thoughtful people living across every border, walking down every street, and working in every city and village. Try to understand and respect them, as you would want them to try to understand and respect you.

4. Stay informed and educate.

Make a concerted effort to fight negative perceptions by being well informed about world history, current affairs in the United States and around the world, and by demonstrating an understanding of other cultures. The knowledge you possess can enlighten the other person.

Can you think of any other strategies?

_____
_____
_____
_____
_____
_____
_____
_____

SELF-CARE SCRIBBLE OR SKETCH!
(use this space to write or draw your thoughts and feelings about **your own self-care**)

NAME:

MY MANY ROLES

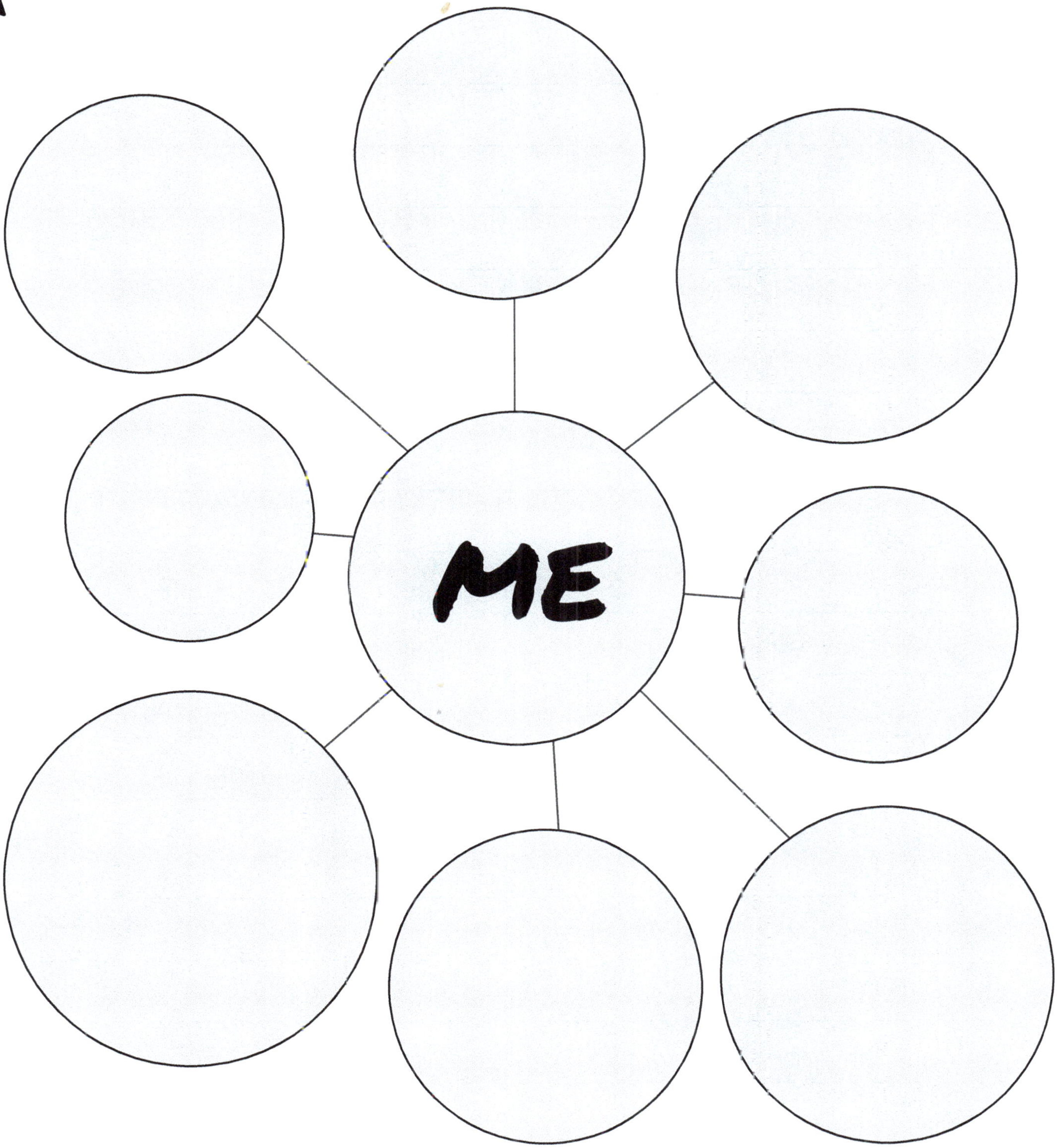

ME

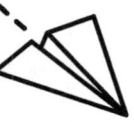 

NAME: _____

ROLE ANALYSIS

Role #1: _____

Description: _____

_____

_____

_____

_____

Role #2: _____

Description: _____

_____

_____

_____

_____

Role #3: _____

Description: _____

_____

_____

_____

_____

NAME:

RELATIONSHIP WEB

Part 1: On the top and bottom or sides of the double lines below, write the name of a person you're in a relationship with and the type of relationship you share (e.g., "Jimmy/Uncle").

Part 2: Next to or on top of the arrow lines, write one word representing how you benefit from that relationship and one way the other person does (e.g., "laughter" for "he makes me laugh," and "love" for "I give him love").

Part 3: On the bottom or inside of the double lines, write one quality of your relationship (e.g., "supportive").

Sample completed relationship arrow:

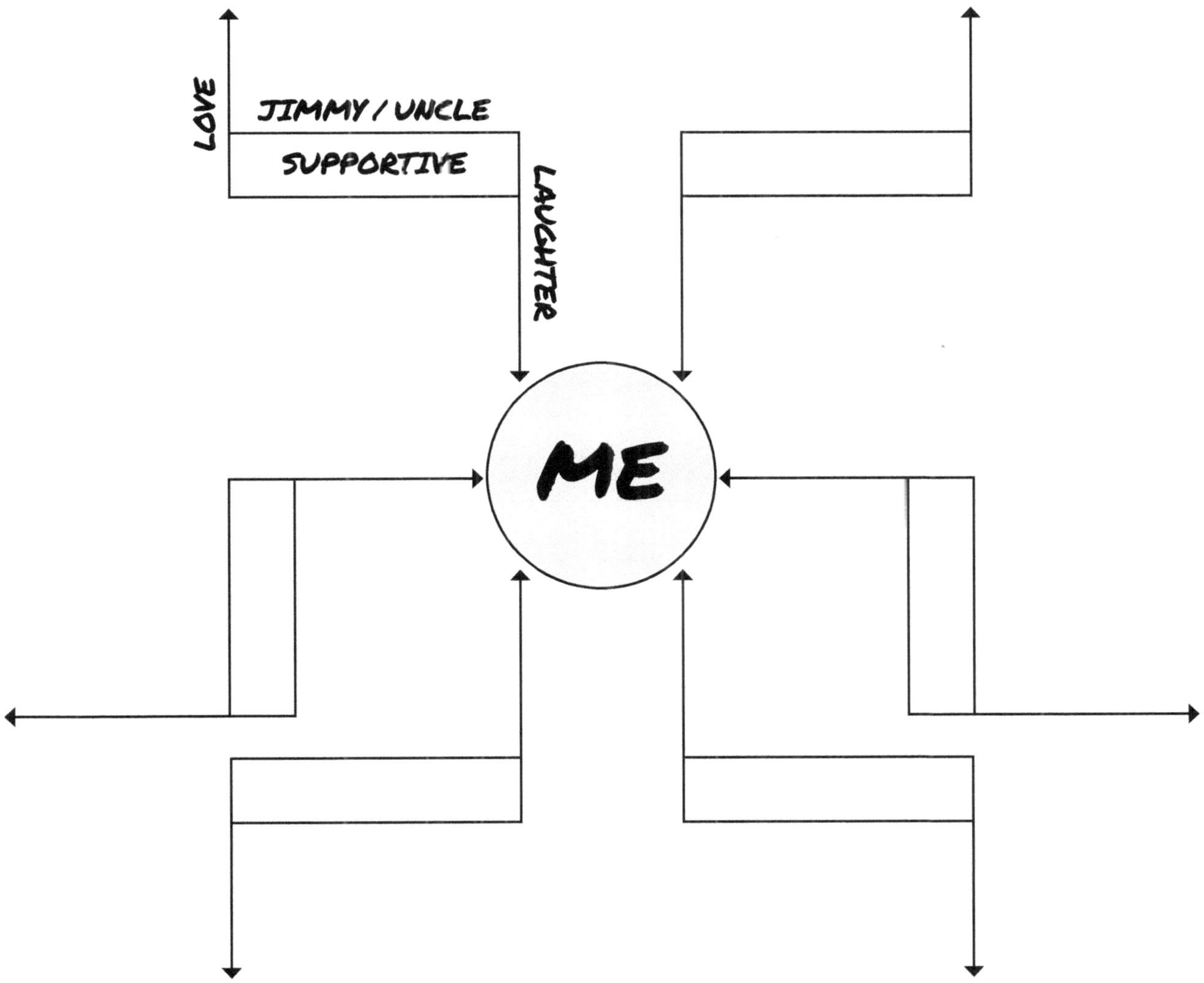

LOVE
JIMMY / UNCLE
SUPPORTIVE
LAUGHTER

ME

NAME: _____

WHO'S THE MAN?

When this saying first appeared, it was a rhetorical question.
One with an answer that was predetermined,
not meant to keep you guessing.
Or an honest quest as to who was the best in the game.
What that game was depended on you,
whether it was on the court, in love,
on the mic, or in school.
What are you expected to do,
what are you forbidden to do,
and what are the rules?
Today we are going to be exploring these issues
thoroughly, most definitely, definitively, through and through . . .

*Complete the following statements
(remember: do whatever's clever but don't take forever).*

PART 1: SENTENCE COMPLETION

A man is _____
A man feels _____
A man should _____
A man cannot _____
A man must _____
A man needs _____
A man wants _____
A man believes _____
A man becomes _____

PART 2: BRAINSTORM

Who's "the man" to you? _____
A man is expected to _____
A man is forbidden to _____

NAME: _____

LYRIC BREAKDOWN

In addition to the following lyrics on being a man by Rodger L. Hilliard, check out the words to the other songs listed below or to some songs you may know.

"Who's the Man?" by Rodger L. Hilliard

How can I blame another man . . . when the guns and drugs are in my brother's hand?
Take a good look at what ya do . . . think real hard who ya doin' it to.
Next one smoked . . . jus' might be you!
I don't need no gun in my hand to be a man . . .
see a brother down . . . reach out . . . give him a hand . . .
show him how to take a stand.
Spread love and peace . . . across the land.
I don't hate the other man . . . I jus' love my brother man.
I don't need to put down no other man . . .
dust off . . . pick up a brother man . .
step right up and be a man . . .
teach love not hate . . . throughout the land . . .
tell me now, my brother . . . do you understand?

Other possibilities for lyrics about being a man:

- "Who's the Man?" by Heavy D
- "I'm the Man" by Chubb Rock
- "Know Thy Self" by KRS-One
- "Who's the Man?" by The Notorious B.I.G.

What do the lyrics of the different songs have in common? Explain and give an example.
_____
_____

How do these lyrics differ from one another? Explain and give an example.
_____
_____

Choose one song you identify with and summarize its message in one sentence.
_____
_____

Is there a music artist today that you feel instructs or addresses men and how they should be and behave? Give an example.
_____
_____

WHAT CONSTITUTES A HEALTHY RELATIONSHIP?

1. **Mutual Respect**—a healthy relationship is built on a foundation of respect for one another, and fosters continued mutual respect in all interactions and communications.

2. **Individual Autonomy**—in a healthy relationship, both parties believe in the other person's right to autonomy. Each person has their own independent friends, tastes, opinions, and interests, and honors the other person's right to have theirs.

3. **Joint Decision Making**—partners in a healthy relationship share the responsibility of making decisions that affect both of them, informing each other of their opinions and preferences, then reaching a conclusion together.

4. **Trust**—in a healthy relationship, people are honest and know they can count on the honesty and integrity of the other person.

5. **Mindful Communication**—in healthy relationships, people can talk about topics that are difficult or sensitive without yelling, blaming each other, or making each other feel guilty.

6. **Negotiation**—in the best of relationships, people don't always have the same opinion or want to do the same things. In healthy relationships, there is room to negotiate so neither partner always gets their choice at the expense of the other; there is give-and-take.

7. **Flex, Not Stress**—healthy relationships cultivate healthy responses to stress. Does one partner need to exercise? Does the other need to chat with friends? Partners in healthy relationships give each other room to de-stress in whatever healthy ways suit them best.

8. **Nonviolent Conflict Resolution**—when conflicts arise in healthy relationships, the partners handle them in a respectful way. A belief in nonviolent conflict resolution means that both partners, no matter how strong their feelings are about something, work toward a resolution without resorting to physical or emotional violence of any kind.

9. **Clear Values and Boundaries**—in healthy relationships, partners respect and maintain each other's boundaries and values, including standards for safe sex and for eliminating behaviors that put either of the partners in discomfort or danger.

10. **Freedom from Substance Abuse**—healthy relationships can only happen when all parties involved are free from drug and alcohol abuse, so that behaviors often associated with relationship violence are taken out of the mix.

Adapted from the CDC (Centers for Disease Control and Prevention) web series Dating Matters: Strategies to Promote Healthy Teen Relationships. See http://www.cdc.gov/ViolencePrevention/pdf/IPV_Strategic_Direction_One-Pager-a.pdf and http://www.cdc.gov/violenceprevention/pdf/dm_overview-a.pdf.

UNHEALTHY RELATIONSHIP WARNING SIGNS!

There are several good sources to help understand what the characteristics of an unhealthy relationship are, and how to spot them. All the sources discuss the following aspects:

- **Abuse** — physical, emotional, sexual, or psychological
- **Unreasonable control** — one person telling the other what he or she can and can't do
- **Constant criticism** — one person making the other feel bad about himself or herself
- **Cutting off** — one person keeping the other isolated from family, friends, or colleagues

THESE FACTORS MAY MANIFEST IN A VARIETY OF BEHAVIORS, INCLUDING:

- 👎 Hurting someone physically
- 👎 Forcing someone to do something he or she doesn't want to do
- 👎 Preventing someone from making his or her own decisions
- 👎 Coercing someone to dress a certain way
- 👎 Ridiculing or putting someone down for their ideas, their looks, their intelligence, their opinions
- 👎 Stopping someone from seeing or spending time with loved ones, including family and friends
- 👎 Insulting someone repeatedly
- 👎 Limiting communications with family, friends, and colleagues, including emails, texting, and phone calls
- 👎 Telling someone they are not capable or worthy
- 👎 Preventing someone from engaging in their choice of activities
- 👎 Keeping someone financially dependent

HOW TO TALK SO TRUSTED ADULTS WILL LISTEN

By now you probably know that communication doesn't always go smoothly. **Emotions** and **past experiences** can get in the way.

Will parents and other trusted adults . . .

- really listen without interrupting?
- take what you say seriously?
- believe you?
- hear you out and respect your opinion?

The answers depend partially on the adults in question, and partially **on you**.

COMMUNICATION IS GIVE-AND-TAKE. YOUR TONE, ATTITUDE, AND LEVEL OF RESPECT CAN INFLUENCE HOW WELL A PARENT OR OTHER TRUSTED ADULT LISTENS TO AND UNDERSTANDS YOU.

Here are some recommendations to keep in mind when talking to adults in your life:

- **Get to the point.** State what you think, feel, and hope for. Give enough clear information to help adults grasp the situation. The more they understand, the more helpful they can be.
- **Be truthful.** If you always tell the truth, adults will be more likely to believe you. If you are known to skip important information or distort facts, adults may not believe what you tell them. If you have lied, they may not trust you.
- **Put yourself in their shoes.** If adults disagree with you, can you understand their perspective? If you can, tell them. Letting adults know you realize they may have different opinions and feelings helps them to be willing to see your point of view.
- **Try not to sound angry or whiny.** Speaking respectfully and pleasantly means adults will be more likely to listen to you and respect what you have to say. And it improves the chances that they'll talk to you respectfully, too. Of course, staying calm can be difficult for any of us (even adults) when we are feeling intense emotions. If there's a possibility that your strong feelings might overwhelm you, do something to work off those feelings before talking: Have a wild dance to your favorite song. Find a noisy place where no one will notice and let out a loud scream. Cry. Hit your pillow. Go for a run. Do whatever you need to do so that you can speak calmly when you need to.

For more tips, go to TeensHealth.org: http://kidshealth.org/en/teens/talk-to-parents.html#

Own Up / Personal Responsibility

NAME: _____

SAY WHAT?

What are you hearing about the groups of people in the left-hand column below?

	At home	At school	From friends	During your commute (walk, subway, bus)
Women				
Men				
Teenagers				
Gays & Lesbians				
People of Color				
Overweight People				
People with Disabilities				

NAME:

MEDALS OF COMPASSION

You have been given one of the five categories of compassion listed below. Think about three "events" of compassion within this category: the individual sprint, the individual marathon, and the team relay.

In the **individual sprint**, consider what kind of compassion someone can show *once*. In the **individual marathon**, consider a *consistent* act of compassion that an individual can show. In the **team relay** category, consider how a *group* can show compassion.

Award gold, silver, and bronze medals in all three events.

What category does your group have? _____
(Categories: Family, Community, Self, Friends, School)

Bronze Medal:

Silver Medal:

Gold Medal:

Bronze Medal:

Silver Medal:

Gold Medal:

Bronze Medal:

Silver Medal:

Gold Medal:

Name: _____

THE TORCH OF COMPASSION BURNS STRONG

Think about a time in your life when you have shown compassion to either yourself, your friends, your school, your family, or your community. Write about that experience next to the torch.

Next, consider how you can keep the "torch of compassion" burning strong. How can you continue to show compassion in your daily life?

_____
_____
_____
_____

OPINION INFLUENCES SCRIBBLE OR SKETCH!
(use this space to write or draw your thoughts and feelings about **the various influences on your opinions and ideas about women and others**)

NAME: _____

Declaration of Respect for Girls and Women

I, _____, in order to create a culture of respect for girls and women, will do the following…

I will _____
_____

I will _____
_____

I will _____
_____

I will _____
_____

I will _____
_____

I will _____
_____

_____   _____
(Student Signature)   (Date)

_____   _____
(Leadership Trainer Signature)   (Date)

PORTRAIT TO IMAGE SAMPLE

Portrait: Here is a portrait I might receive . . .

Image: Here are two images I might create to represent this portrait . . .

Name: _____

IDEAS + IMAGES

1. What feeling or emotion would you associate with this image?
_____
_____
_____

2. What aspects of this image are appealing to you?
_____
_____
_____

3. What aspects of this image would you change?
_____
_____
_____

4. What would you imagine were some of the qualities of the original portrait?
_____
_____
_____

NAME:

WHAT'S MY STYLE?

Please answer the questions truthfully and quickly; don't think about them too much. Just go with your first thought.

PART 1: PEOPLE-TO-PEOPLE STYLE OF LEARNING: PEOPLE ORIENTED

1) How did it feel to share with everyone?

2) What did you like about the exercise?

Part 1 rating from 1 to 10 (1 = hated it! 10 = loved it!) Rating _____

PART 2: COOPERATION-TOSS STYLE OF LEARNING: BODY ORIENTED

1) How did it feel to try to keep track of many different balls?

2) What did you like about the exercise?

Part 2 rating from 1 to 10 (1 = hated it! 10 = loved it!) Rating _____

NAME:

PART 3: TEASE MY BRAIN! STYLE OF LEARNING: NUMBER ORIENTED

1) What are some of the feelings that came up while you were filling out the worksheet?

2) What did you like about the exercise?

Part 3 rating from 1 to 10 (1 = hated it! 10 = loved it!) Rating _____

PART 4: FUTURE ME! STYLE OF LEARNING: PICTURE ORIENTED

1) How did it feel to make a drawing of your future?

2) What did you like about the exercise?

Part 4 rating from 1 to 10 (1 = hated it! 10 = loved it!) Rating _____

PART 5: MY-BACKPACK STYLE OF LEARNING: SELF ORIENTED

1) How did it feel to think about the qualities you possess?

2) What did you like about the exercise?

Part 5 rating from 1 to 10 (1 = hated it! 10 = loved it!) Rating _____

NAME:

PART 6: TELEPHONE RACE / WORD-SEARCH STYLE OF LEARNING: WORD ORIENTED

1) How did it feel to have to remember a sentence? How easy or difficult was it to complete the word search?

2) What did you like about the exercise?

Part 6 rating from 1 to 10 (1 = hated it! 10 = loved it!) Rating _____

PART 7: TWINKLE, TWINKLE REMIX STYLE OF LEARNING: MUSIC ORIENTED

1) How did it feel to make music?

2) What did you like about the exercise?

Part 7 rating from 1 to 10 (1 = hated it! 10 = loved it!) Rating _____

Now take a look at all the activities and the styles they represent.
Then look at your ratings, think about what you experienced, and choose
the learning style or styles that you enjoyed the most!

That's your style!

NAME: _____

TEASE MY BRAIN!

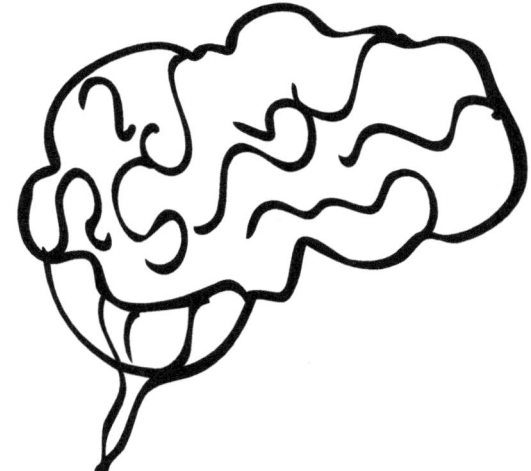

All of Jenny's pets are dogs except one. All of her pets are cats except one. How many cats and dogs does Jenny have?

Answer_____

NAME:

MY BACKPACK

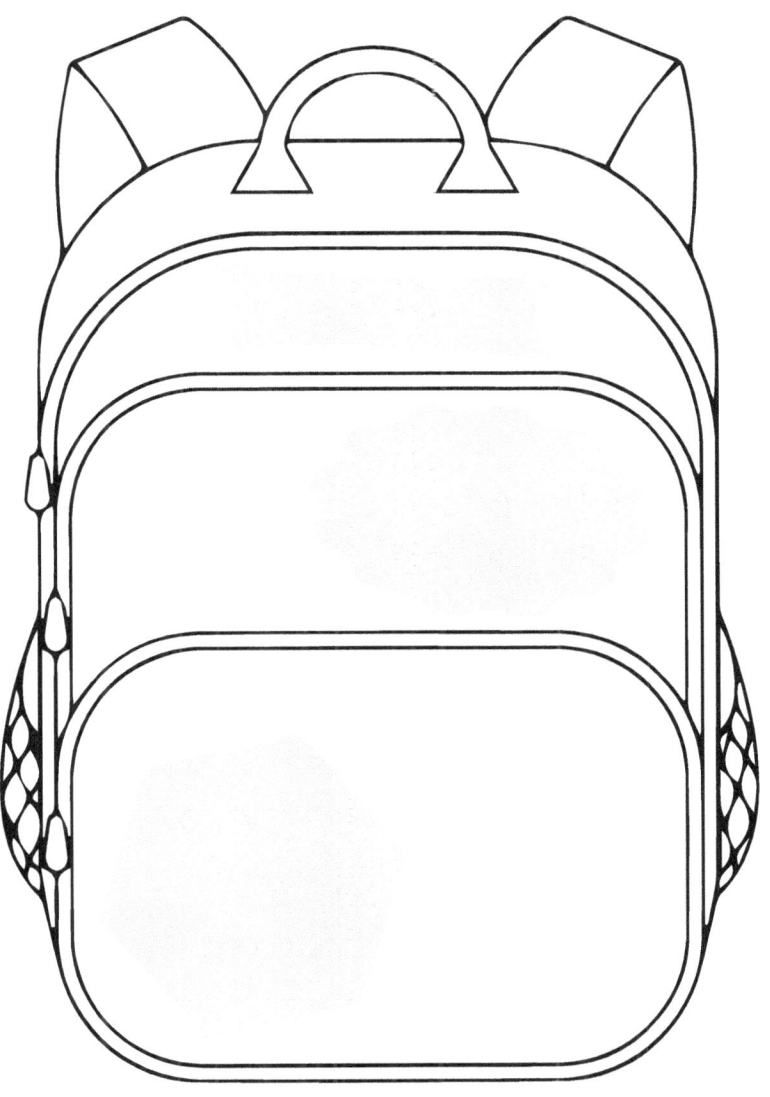

It's a big school, and there are lots of students with lots of backpacks. Just as in life, there are lots of different people with lots of different personalities. If your backpack represented your life, the things that you kept inside it and the way you decorated the outside would help define who you are as a person.

List three physical items that someone would find in your backpack that would help identify you as the owner.

Example: If you are a football player, they might find a football.

1.

2.

3.

Now list three characteristics of your personality that would define who you are as a person on the stickers outside your bag.

Example: If you are really courageous, you could have a sticker with the word "Brave" written on it.

How did it feel to think about the things that define you as a person?

_____

_____

_____

_____

NAME: _____

WHAT'S THE MESSAGE?

```
J C F R A U Q H H D X V P U S E X X U K
J J O F N Z O Y Z J M V C Q E Z V M X C
G K M Z K F K J Q D A B M A G V J X B C
W N C T R Z D J U E K K L W C F B C C W
N I P S C N I Q E H K Z T K P D J J I R
Q C P O G H Y S H U R H E Q U R C Y N X
L K R J S N U E F R E H L M Q M T C Q T
T S N F R R I W R I M K B S N T W V L E
Q I T M L F Z K I I Y B Z E L P R U P W
M A G A U Y C L C O P I R Y Y F J V N U
Z A W N Q G X I N O F Z M L Z E A P Y W
M A Y Y W R C S D A T F U L B Y H N Z J
N Y V J T N F P M J C S P I B Y J T O N
X Q R D H A O Z J Z J C D W T N Q S G T
B J H O J K O N Z Y Q Y G O L D X M A S
T D U L W X K Y K D Z A Y R N Q T O M T
O X T U U R D C C T A G K E A F Z O E H
V W X E J A A A I S S R P Y D F A M F M
Z X D S M W F N C G O K J W R X Q A M I
A I J Z B A E V O I T W D O I Y C V G O
```

What was the correct telephone message? Write it in the blanks below, one word per line:

_____ _____ _____ _____ _____

_____ _____ _____ _____ _____ _____.

Now find each of the words in the word search above and circle them!

50

TWINKLE, TWINKLE, LITTLE STAR

Twinkle Twinkle Little Star
How I wonder what you are
Up above the world so high
Like a diamond in the sky
Twinkle Twinkle Little Star
How I wonder what you are

NAME:

LEARNING STYLES: WHAT KIND OF LEARNER ARE YOU?

There are many different ways to learn, and we all have different styles. Some of us are more physical, and some of us like music. Some of us love words, and others like to draw. We're all different, and that's okay!

Do you like to talk to others? Do you like to meet new people? Do you like to learn new things about people? Do you belong to a lot of clubs or activities? Do you enjoy putting together parties or events? Do you like to tell stories? Do you enjoy getting attention from your peers? Can you read people's moods and emotions easily?	Maybe You Are An Interpersonal Learner! *"People Oriented"*	Study Tip: *Create a study buddy group.* What else could you try?
Do you like to dance? Do you like to act? Do you enjoy games like charades? Do you like to play sports or exercise? Do you enjoy scavenger hunts? Do you like to bounce balls or move around while you are listening or studying? Do you find it hard to sit still? Do you like to go on walks?	Maybe You Are A Bodily/Kinesthetic Learner! *"Body Oriented"*	Study Tip: *Take frequent stretch breaks when you study. Read your homework chapters aloud.* What else could you try?
Do you enjoy math? Do you play sudoku? Can you find patterns in things? Do you like to solve riddles? Are you interested in the stock market? Do you like money? Do you like symbols? Do you like games such as Monopoly? Do you play chess? Do you follow sports statistics, like batting averages? Do you make Pros and Cons lists? Can you easily follow recipes?	Maybe You Are A Logical/ Mathematical Learner! *"Number Oriented"*	Study Tip: *Break your notes up into diagrams or tips.* What else could you try?

Study Tip: *Draw pictures to remember stories or information.* What else could you try?

Study Tip: *Set aside time every morning to journal about the day ahead.* What else could you try?

Study Tip: *Read your homework chapters aloud.* What else could you try?

Study Tip: *Write a song or a rap to help you remember information.* What else could you try?

Maybe You Are A Visual/Spatial Learner!

"Picture Oriented"

Maybe You Are An Intrapersonal Learner!

"Self Oriented"

Maybe You Are A Verbal/Linguistic Learner!

"Word Oriented"

Maybe You Are A Musical/Rhythmic Learner!

"Music Oriented"

Do you doodle while you are talking on the phone? Do you sketch or draw things while listening to people talk? Do you enjoy making collages? Do you like to draw? Are you interested in art? Do you like color? Do you like games like Pictionary? Do you take photographs? Do you like posters and pictures on the wall? When you read, do you imagine the characters in your head?

Do you like to keep a journal? Do you enjoy spending time alone? Do you like to play games like Concentration? Do you have an active imagination? Do you spend a lot of time thinking about your future and setting goals for yourself? Do you feel like you are self-aware and can understand your own moods and feelings?

Do you like words? Do you like to read? Do you remember things that people tell you? Can you express yourself well when you speak? Do you write poetry or raps? Do you like to do crossword puzzles? Do you do word searches?

Do you play a musical instrument? Do you like to listen to music? Do you like to dance? Do you sing? Do you like to listen to the sounds of the city? Does listening to music help you concentrate? Do you whistle or hum? Do you think of a song to match different moments in your life?

NAME:

ACTION PLAN IN ACTION EXAMPLE

Topic: Gaming

Ways to learn more about this area:

- Follow a gaming blog.
- Follow a game-making company on Twitter.
- Use online programs to make games.
- Reserve computer time in the lab.
- Ask my teacher about e-sports.

The strategy I will use to further my knowledge in this area:

- I will reserve computer time in the lab every Monday and Wednesday during lunch period.
- I will start following Riot Games Inc. on Twitter and check the feed every day after school.
- Tomorrow, during lunch, I will ask my teacher about e-sports.

The ways I will know that my strategy worked:

- By next week, I will know how to get involved in e-sports.
- In two weeks, I will know five different pieces of information about how games are made.
- In one month, I will have created a small web-based game.

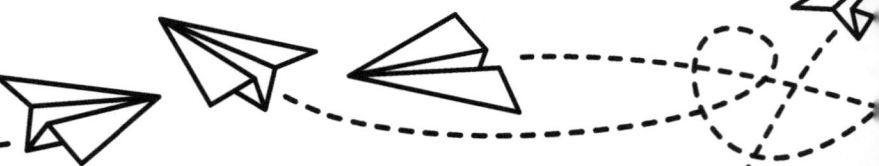

NAME: _____

ACTION PLAN IN ACTION

Topic:

Ways to learn more about this area:

-
-
-
-
-

The strategy I will use to further my knowledge in this area:

-
-
-
-
-

The ways I will know that my strategy worked:

-
-
-

NAME: _____

MY IDEAL NEIGHBORHOOD

Working with your group, complete this form to design an **Ideal Neighborhood**. If you had your wish, how would you want your neighborhood to look? Write about or draw your answers in the spaces below.

Neighborhood Name	
What businesses would be in your neighborhood?	
What would the streets and sidewalks look like?	
What would your building or the ground that your house sits on look like (including hallways and walkways of building)?	
Describe the sounds and smells	
Describe any community or recreational spaces or events	
Other resources that would make your ideal neighborhood great might be _____	

NAME:

WHAT'S YOUR PLAN FOR CHANGE?

You can make change in your own neighborhood. And you can make that change now. Below, fill in the prompts of what change you are going to make and how you'll go about making that change. Remember to choose something that is realistic and to give yourself a deadline.

WHAT DO YOU WANT TO CHANGE/CREATE IN YOUR NEIGHBORHOOD?

HOW WILL YOU GO ABOUT DOING THIS?

HOW LONG WILL IT TAKE TO ACCOMPLISH THIS GOAL?

WHO CAN HELP YOU COMPLETE THIS CHANGE?

NAME: _____

IMMEDIATE ACTIONS, LONG-TERM EFFECTS

For each situation, write down an immediate action you can take to respond. Then, write down what potential long-term effect your immediate action might have. An example has been provided to guide you.

SCENARIO	IMMEDIATE ACTION	LONG-TERM EFFECT
Example: *You witness a student being bullied in your classroom.*	**Example:** *You stand up for that student.*	**Example:** *That student builds confidence and eventually stands up for him/herself.*
You witness a pregnant woman standing while you are seated on the train.		
You notice that the new student in your school is lost and cannot find his/her next class.		
The cashier at the grocery store gives you too much change back.		
Your best friend decides he/she is going to cut class today.		
Create your own:		
Create your own:		

NAME:

SCHOOL SERVICE TAKEOVER TASKS

Write down the specific actions you take to serve your school during the group walk in the table below.

ACT OF SERVICE	SERVICE RECIPIENTS
Example: *Picked up bag of potato chips from floor.*	Example: *School cafeteria. Everyone who eats in the cafeteria. Custodian.*

COMMUNITY SERVICE SCRIBBLE OR SKETCH!

(use this space to write or draw your thoughts and feelings about **participating in community service**)

Man Up / My Roles as a Man

WHAT'S IN A NAME?

Many names have special significance, sometimes culturally, sometimes personally. Here is a list of names with their cultural meanings.

Aaron	Mountain of strength
Abdul	Servant of God
Earl	A noted warrior
Eggert	As strong as the edge of a sword
Jabari	Courageous
Khari	Like a king
Nuru	Filled with light
Ramon	Wise protector
Utku	Victorious
Walden	Forest valley
Wang	Royal or imperial

NAME:

MY FAVORITE TV DAD

Take two minutes to write down your favorite TV dad with a brief explanation for why and post it on the corresponding box below.

Black-ish

George Lopez

Fresh Off the Boat

The Cosby Show

Modern Family

NAME:

HisSTORY PROFILE

Answer the questions below according to what you saw in the HisStory testimonial videos.

1. One quality of a person's character that I think makes them a good father is:

2. One example of how that character quality makes someone a good father is:

3. One thing that was said in the videos that affected me was:

4. Who or what do I think shaped this person's ideas about fatherhood?:

5. If there were one message in the videos about being a father I would want to pass on as a legacy to other potential fathers, I think it would be:

NAME: _____

MY VISION STATEMENT

Take the following steps to help develop your own vision statement as a father figure.

STEP 1: Project into the future a clear image of who you want/need to be as a father figure.
STEP 2: Dream big and focus on success.
STEP 3: Use the present tense, imagining yourself already in the future.
STEP 4: Fill in your vision statement with passion and emotion.
STEP 5: Plan to communicate your vision statement to others.
STEP 6: Be prepared to commit time and resources to the vision you establish.

MY VISION STATEMENT

> Write a vision statement for yourself as a future father figure here.

THE FIVE WORLDS OF SUCCESS

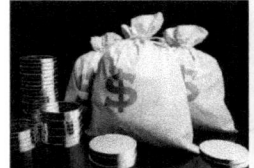    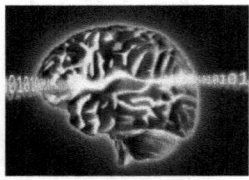

Material	Spiritual	Emotional	Physical	Mental
Financial security	Sharing knowledge	Relationships	Strength	Mastering yourself
Living in a luxurious house	Journey	Happiness	Freedom	Competence
Jewelry	Independence	Being well-liked	Flexibility	Overcoming fear or adversity
New cars	Access to nature	Making friends	Travel	Staying positive
Fancy clothes	Helping others	Having a family	Hobbies	Never giving up
Influence	Enjoying your work	Feeling useful	Leisure time	Utilizing your talents and skills
High income	Finding your purpose	Working effectively with others	Hard work	Sense of duty
Perks and bonuses	Peace	Endurance	Open space	Focus
Home	Simplicity	Satisfaction	Discipline	Confidence
Recognition	Being creative	Feeling victorious	Living in a clean, safe environment	Intelligence
TOTAL POINTS:	TOTAL POINTS:	TOTAL POINTS:	TOTAL POINTS:	TOTAL POINTS:

SUCCESSFUL MAN SCRIBBLE OR SKETCH!
(use this space to write or draw your thoughts and feelings about **becoming a successful man**)

TALKING TO AUTHORITY FIGURES SCRIBBLE OR SKETCH!
(use this space to write or draw your thoughts and feelings about **talking to authority figures**)

DEALING WITH DISAPPOINTMENT SCRIBBLE OR SKETCH!
(use this space to write or draw your thoughts and feelings about **dealing with disappointment**)

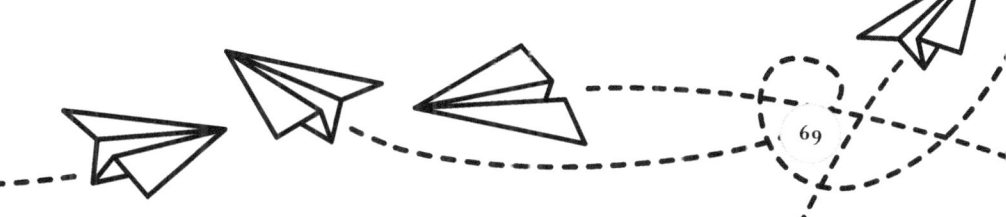

SPEAKING WITH AUTHORITY FIGURES

1. **Remember that the person in authority was like you once.** All authority figures were once kids, and all of them have been talked to by someone they saw as an authority figure.

   - Some authority figures may use scare tactics as a way of trying to control others. The important word here is "trying"; they can only control you or frighten you if you let them. Stay calm and assertive—not aggressive—when facing people who try to scare you.

2. **Put a hold on defensiveness.** It's easy to get defensive and pass the blame or refuse to take responsibility. But defensiveness takes a lot of energy, can block you from hearing the real message and can make you seem guilty, even when you aren't.

3. **Answer questions at appropriate times.** Don't interrupt the other person with your answer before they've finished asking the question. If you do so, you will seem either suspicious, aggressive, or rudely overconfident about yourself.

   - Sometimes authority figures can be harsh in asking questions, causing you to react out of fear, anxiety, or anger. Be sure to catch yourself: breathe and answer the questions. Listen well so you don't mistake rhetorical questions (that is, questions you're not really expected to answer, like "What were you thinking?") for questions you should answer.

4. **Don't take a step back.** Often, when we talk to authority figures, we physically back up. This is instinctual for humans—if we feel we're about to be attacked, we automatically step back to avoid a blow. Stand up for yourself confidently. Make sure you *respectfully* stand your ground with the authority figure.

5. **Control your nervousness.** For some people, seeing a uniform or the official title on a person's badge or door is enough to make them shake, but controlling your nervousness is very important. Focus on breathing deeply, taking slow and gentle breaths directly from your diaphragm. This will reduce your nervousness and start to relax you. Take everything slowly, even if the authority figure appears to want immediate responses.

6. **Trust in the intention of the authority figure to be a guide or mentor.** If you're in a situation where the authority figure is calling out your behavior or attitude issues, see this as a learning opportunity. Often people in authority are in a position to see things that you can't, and they are trying, in their own way, to guide you and keep you from repeating avoidable mistakes.

7. **Focus on the positive.** Accept that your principal, teacher, mentor, or other authority figure has a point. Rather than trying to avoid blame or make awkward excuses, focus on what you *can* do to improve the situation from this point on. This will show the authority figure that you're stepping up to their challenge or accepting their points and that you're willing to find solutions.

8. **Stand up to the authority figure when necessary.** This step isn't relevant unless you're being pushed around in a serious situation, in particular one where you could potentially be suspended, receive punishment, or even lose privileges or your freedom. If blamed for something you didn't do, clearly and calmly state, without interrupting, "I didn't do that." However . . .

   - Don't deny what you know is true.
   - If you are at fault for something, accept the blame and offer to do what's necessary to make amends. Always take responsibility if it was you who did something wrong or you who made a poor judgment call.

Adapted from http://www.wikihow.com/Talk-to-Authority

Rise Up / Future Plans

RESPONDING TO FAILURE SCRIBBLE OR SKETCH!

(use this space to write or draw your thoughts and feelings about **not succeeding at something you try**)

Name:

NO PROBLEM! (SAMPLE PROBLEM)

1. WHAT'S THE PROBLEM OR QUESTION?

What is my attitude toward this problem? *I want to further my education, but I am scared of moving away from home. I don't like change.*

What are the personal values that will be involved with this decision? *I value a good education. I value being able to support myself.*

What is my decision-making goal? *To have a good-paying job.*

Whom have I talked to? *My mother, the career counselor, and my English teacher.*

The problem: *Should I go to college in the fall?*

2. IMPORTANT OR UNIMPORTANT: YOU DECIDE

Is this problem important or unimportant? *Very important.*

Why? *It will have a big effect on my future.*

3. GATHER AND ANALYZE THE INFO: WHAT'S THE 411?

Facts: *Out-of-state tuition is $30,000/year, travel time is three hours, school near home does not specialize in my major, no friends at out-of-state school, lots of friends at school near home, offered a low-paying job after high school graduation, parents want me to go to college near home, can get student loan, etc.*

4. DEVELOP PLANS A, B, AND C; THEN CHOOSE ONE

Plan A: *Go away to college in the fall.*   Plan B: *Go to college near my home.*

Plan C: *Stay home and get a job.*   My decision: *Go away to college.*

5. NOW DO SOMETHING: TAKE ACTION

Action Steps: 1. *Apply to out-of-state school.*
2. *Research financial aid.*
3. *Visit out-of-state school on a weekend.*

6. YOU DECIDED. WHAT HAPPENED? NOW EVALUATE

What are the results of my decision? *I have been accepted to out-of-state school*

Do I want to change my action? *No, but I need to find more resources for financial aid.*

NAME:

NO PROBLEM!

1. WHAT'S THE PROBLEM OR QUESTION?

What is my attitude toward this problem?

What are the personal values that will be involved with this decision?

What is my decision-making goal?

Whom have I talked to?

The problem:

2. IMPORTANT OR UNIMPORTANT: YOU DECIDE

Is this problem important or unimportant?

Why?

3. GATHER AND ANALYZE THE INFO: WHAT'S THE 411?

Brainstorm all the facts around this problem.

Research the facts.

4. DEVELOP PLANS A, B, AND C; THEN CHOOSE ONE

Plan A: Plan B:

Plan C: My decision:

5. NOW DO SOMETHING: TAKE ACTION

Action Steps: 1.
               2.
               3.

6. YOU DECIDED. WHAT HAPPENED? NOW EVALUATE

What are the results of my decision?

Do I want to change my action?

NAME:

CHOICES, DECISIONS, CONSEQUENCES (SAMPLE MODEL)

Situation: Friends tell you another student has been spreading terrible rumors about you.

Choices	Decisions	Consequences
Fight Ignore it Spread rumors about them Tell a teacher or trusted adult Confront them	Fight	Get hurt Get suspended Get props for being tough
	Ignore it	Rumors stop Rumors get worse Stay in school
	Spread rumors about them	Hurt feelings Physical violence Suspension
	Tell a teacher or trusted adult	Rumors stop Other students call you "snitch" Nothing changes
	Confront them	Hurt Feelings Resolved and Rumors Stop Anger Rumors get worse

NAME:

TO BLANK OR NOT TO BLANK

1. Write down all the decisions that you make today, and document as many as you can in the space below. Also, document the consequences of those decisions.

2. In the first column, put an "X" by the decisions that you really thought about and an "O" next to the decisions that were made out of habit or without thinking.

3. Next, put an asterisk (*) by the decisions that had positive consequences.

4. Finally, answer the questions at the bottom.

X or O?	Decision	Consequence

Is there any relationship between the consequences and the decisions? If yes, why do you think so?

Did your attitude, values, and goals have anything to do with whether a decision received an "X" or an "O"?

What can you do to make more decisions with positive consequences?

Name: _____

C, D, C—SETTING THE SCENE

Who are your characters?:

CHARACTER 1

Name: _____

Age: _____

Occupation: _____

Favorite thing to do: _____

CHARACTER 2

Name: _____

Age: _____

Occupation: _____

Favorite thing to do: _____

Do they know each other? If so, what is their relationship? _____
_____

Where does the scene take place? _____
_____

What is the situation? _____
_____
_____
_____
_____

NAME:

WHAT'S MY GOAL?

Use the spaces below to brainstorm both your long-term and your short-term goals. Don't limit yourself; write down as many goals as you can think of. Think about goals for school, career, friends and family, hobbies, personal health and wellness, and so on.

LONG-TERM GOALS:

Example: I want to graduate from college.

SHORT-TERM GOALS:

Example: I want to get all As on my next report card.

NAME: _____

HOW DO I GET WHERE I'M GOING?

One of my biggest long-term goals:

Some short-term goals that will help me achieve this:

The four biggest obstacles to achieving my goal:

1. _____
_____
2. _____
_____
3. _____
_____
4. _____
_____

NAME:

Advice from classmates:

Action plan:

Steps I have taken this week toward achieving my goals:

NAME:

PYRAMID OF SUCCESS

Vision:

Goal:

_____

_____

_____

Strategy:

_____

_____

_____

Actions:

_____

_____

_____

NAME: _____

VISION PAGE

1. Getting Started at College	2. Academic Success

3. Social Success	4. College Graduation

NAME: _____

MY IDEAL ROOMMATE

Think about what it would be like to share a room with someone you don't know well. That's what it's like to have a college roommate. What things would be helpful to know about yourself, so you can find a good match in a roommate?

1. In the table below, circle all that apply to you in the Preferences/Options column.
2. Then rate your circled preferences/options in each Habit category, with 1 being your first choice.

Habit	I See Myself …	Preferences/Options	Priorities
Study Habits:	Studying where:	My room	
		The library	
		Other:	
	Studying when:	Mornings	
		Afternoons	
		Evenings	
		Late nights	
		Other:	
Living Habits:	Keeping my living space:	Fairly neat	
		Messy	
		Organized	
		Other:	
	Listening to music:	Hip-hop	
		Classic rock	
		R & B	
		Pop	
		Other genres:	
		With headphones	
		Without headphones	
Sleep Habits:	Going to sleep:	9:00–10:00 p.m.	
		10:00–11:00 p.m.	
		11:00 p.m.–midnight	
		After midnight	
		With windows open	
		With windows closed	
		And sleeping through any noise around me	
		And being disturbed by noise in the room	

NAME:

Habit	I See Myself …	Preferences/Options	Priorities
Personal Habits:	Spending my free time:	Watching movies	
		Listening to music	
		Going out with friends	
		Playing video games	
		Playing sports	
		Going to school events (concerts, festivals, games)	
		Doing community service	
		Other:	

3. What else might be helpful to know about yourself in figuring out who would be a good match in a roommate? Write about other preferences and habits that might make a difference:

_____
_____
_____
_____
_____
_____
_____
_____

4. Note anything else you want to keep in mind for a future roommate in the section below:

_____
_____
_____
_____
_____
_____
_____
_____

NAME: _____

DREAM JOB REQUIREMENTS

WHAT'S REQUIRED OF ME IN THIS POSITION?

1. In the bigger cloud below, write your dream job.
2. In the surrounding clouds, list what you think you need to do in order to be considered a model employee.

NAME: _____

CAREER PURSUIT

Is going into a career because he can make a lot of money in this field	Wants to practice his career outside of the state where he lives	Knows someone who is in the career I want to go into	Wants to go into the same career as a family member
Knows what he wants to be when he grows up	Will wait until he gets into college to figure out a career	Is going into a career because it's fun	Knows what college to go to that specializes in his career field
Has visited an establishment that houses the career he wants	Wants to be famous from his career	Volunteers somewhere	Has chosen a career because his parents told him to go into it

IDEAL LEGACY SCRIBBLE OR SKETCH!
(use this space to write or draw your thoughts and feelings about **your ideal legacy**)

DREAM IMAGE JOB OPENING

DREAM IMAGE

WHO WE ARE:

Dream Image is a new arts-in-education organization that integrates the arts into the curricula of high school students. We train professional artists to work side by side with classroom teachers to help students write and perform their own stories. Dream Image helps young people develop their creativity and their own voices, bringing positive change to their communities and society as a whole.

JOB OPENING: OFFICE MANAGER

DUTIES INCLUDE:

- Serving as a receptionist and answering multiline phone system
- Recording inventory and ordering supplies
- Running a monthly payroll for a staff of up to fifty artists
- Filing and mailing

ADDITIONAL QUALIFICATIONS:

- Proficient in MS Word, Excel, and FileMaker
- Highly organized
- Strong writing and verbal skills
- Able to handle several tasks at once
- Work independently and as part of a team
- Flexible and able to take initiative

HOW TO APPLY:

Please send résumé, cover letter, and salary requirements to Jonathan Winn at [contact info].

INTERVIEW DOS AND DON'TS

DOs	DON'Ts
Wear a suit (navy, gray, or charcoal) or neatly pressed light-colored shirt and neutral slacks.	Avoid clothing with political or social commentary or images that could be offensive to someone.
Keep ties, shoes, and socks relatively conservative.	Avoid dry hands. Clean and lightly moisturize your hands and face before you leave your house.
Trim hair collar-length or shorter and wear it neatly groomed.	Avoid having cracked or peeling lips. Exfoliate and moisturize with lip balm.
Shave or neatly trim facial hair.	Do not leave more than one shirt button open. Trim any excess hair that appears outside the neckline.
Practice good hygiene and bathe carefully.	Do not wear your nails too long. Keep them clean and trimmed.
Brush and floss your teeth. Check the mirror before you reach your interview destination.	Do not arrive late for the interview. Show up fifteen minutes early and calmly review your credentials.
Maintain eye contact. Smile.	Do not sit with your legs too far apart. Maintain a comfortable seated position.
Listen carefully to the interviewer's questions. Answer the questions in a clear and thoughtful manner.	Do not shuffle disorganized papers during the interview. Come prepared with a folder, a pen, and notepaper, plus copies of your résumé and references.
Have a firm handshake (but don't overdo it).	Don't use excessive hand gestures.

FINAL REFLECTIONS SCRIBBLE OR SKETCH!

(use this space to write or draw your thoughts and feelings about **your experience in this program/club**)

REFERENCE

Credits

IMAGES

All images are via Shutterstock unless otherwise noted.

Design elements used throughout: © Bokica, © aunaauna, © bounward, © Vector Tradition SM, © Dacian G, © Keep Calm and Vector, © dbambic/Pixabay, © Ui Parade/Caboozi, © Clker-Free-Vector-Images/Pixabay, © metsi/Pixabay; © raniramli/Pixabay; © OpenClipart-Vectors/Pixabay.

Cover: © Bokica/Shutterstock; © EstherQueen999/Shutterstock.

Interior: p. 12: © OpenClipart-Vectors/Pixabay; p. 13: © Clker-Free-Vector-Images/Pixabay; p. 18: © OpenClipart-Vectors/Pixabay; p. 22: © OpenClipart-Vectors/Pixabay; p. 23: © OpenClipart-Vectors/Pixabay, © Clker-Free-Vector-Images/Pixabay; p. 24: © metsi/Pixabay; p. 27: © kropekk_pl/Pixabay; p. 30: © Rawpixel.com; p. 32: © OpenClipart-Vectors/Pixabay; p. 33: © Clker-Free-Vector-Images/Pixabay; p. 34: © OpenClipart-Vectors/Pixabay; p. 35: © AtStock Productions; p. 36: © OpenClipart-Vectors/Pixabay; p. 39: © bartekhdd/Pixabay; p. 40: © OpenClipart-Vectors/Pixabay; p. 43: © Eugene Powers, © Macrovector; p. 49: © yuelanliu/Pixabay; p. 51: © Dacian G/Shutterstock; p. 52: © univfajar/Pixabay, © maxlkt/Pixabay, © GDJ/Pixabay; p. 53: © rawpixel/Pixabay, © Free-Photos/Pixabay, © OpenClipart-Vectors/Pixabay; p. 54: © metsi/Pixabay; p. 57: © OpenIcons/Pixabay; p. 64: © OpenClipart-Vectors/Pixabay; p. 65: © OpenClipart-Vectors/Pixabay; p. 76: © OpenClipart-Vectors/Pixabay; p. 77: © OpenClipart-Vectors/Pixabay; p. 78: © OpenClipart-Vectors/Pixabay, © Clker-Free-Vector-Images/Pixabay; p. 79: © OpenClipart-Vectors/Pixabay; p. 80: © Clker-Free-Vector-Images/Pixabay; p. 81: © Keep Calm and Vector/Shutterstock; p. 82: © kropekk_pl/Pixabay; p. 85: © Clker-Free-Vector-Images/Pixabay.

REFERENCE

About The Leadership Program

OUR VISION

We create experiences that inspire people to step into their leadership and make positive change in their lives and in the world.

WHO WE ARE

For over twenty years, The Leadership Program has worked to provide youth development activities and parent and professional development workshops and coaching.

The Leadership Program believes that with the right help, every person has the innate ability to lead the change.

For more information about Leadership Program publications and programs, visit our website at http://tlpnyc.com or contact us at info@tlpnyc.com.

Other program curriculum support available from The Leadership Program at www.tlpnyc.com/leadership-marketplace.

Boys 2 MENtors: Curriculum Manual

HERstory: Curriculum Suite

HERstory: Student Writing Companion

Empowering Upstanders: A School-Based Bullying Prevention Program

Empowering Upstanders: Student Workbook

Leadership Skills: High School Manual: Violence Prevention Project

Leadership Skills: High School Workbook: Violence Prevention Project

Leadership Skills: Middle School Workbook: Violence Prevention Project

Leadership Skills: Middle School Manual: Violence Prevention Project

www.ingramcontent.com/pod-product-compliance
Lightning Source LLC
Chambersburg PA
CBHW081841170426
43199CB00017B/2809